Scary Cute

25 Amigurumi Monsters to Make

Annie Obaachan

APPLE

A QUANTUM BOOK

First published in the UK in 2011 by
Apple Press
7 Greenland Street
London NW1 OND
United Kingdom
www.apple-press.com

Copyright © Quantum Publishing Ltd 2010

This book is conceived, designed and produced by
Quantum Publishing Ltd
6 Blundell Street
London N7 9BH

ISBN: 978 1 84543 404 5

QUMSC2A

Printed and bound in Singapore

Design: Wei Chong
Photographer: Marcos Bevilacqua
Managing Editor: Julie Brooke
Project Editor: Samantha Warrington
Assistant Editor: Jo Morley
Production Manager: Rohana Yusof
Publisher: Sarah Bloxham

Contents

Cute, Cute, Cute

Welcome to the Wonderful World of **Amigurumi**

What is amigurumi?

The word *amigurumi* is a combination of the words *ami* and *nuigurumi*. *Ami* means 'knit/crochet' in Japanese and *nuigurumi* means 'stuffed toy'. Put them together, and you have a crocheted stuffed toy.

No one really knows where amigurumi came from. There have always been handmade toys in Japan. Japan has a rich history in textiles, as we can see in weaving for kimonos, the Japanese traditional costume. But there is no such history of knitting or crochet. The Japanese simply took these Western crafts and, instead of using them for purely functional items like socks and scarves, started to create little animals. Nowadays there are hundreds of amigurumi exhibitions and clubs, not only in Japan but all over the world.

The birth of amigurumi may have been greatly influenced by Japanese traditional doll culture, which has a long history. Hina Matsuri, a doll festival in honour of Girls' Day, is celebrated on the third of March every year, just in time for the peach blossoms. The Odairi-sama/Ohina-sama dolls, representing the Emperor and the Empress, are displayed for this festival by each family with a daughter to ensure her future happiness. This set of dolls tends to be handed down from generation to generation with love, respect and a sense of history. Boys also have a special doll festival in May.

The dolls stay with Japanese children all their lives, lifting their spirits in times of stress and trouble. Amigurumi animals are an extension of this doll culture, brightening up cloudy days and providing a source of comfort at the toughest of times.

The last few years have witnessed a flowering of Japanese subcultures worldwide. A particularly popular feature of this phenomenon is the Japanese kawaii culture. The closest translation of *kawaii* in English is 'cute'. From Hello Kitty to Pokémon, anime to manga, cute Japanese characters have swarmed across the world and conquered our hearts. Amigurumi creations also swam with this kawaii-tide. Small, cute and easy to make, how could they fail to captivate us?

In Japan, people like to keep these animals with them throughout the day. You will see them hanging off bags next to lucky charms, or sitting atop computers and piles of work in the office. Amigurumi characters can comfort and reassure us in this hectic world, secretly saying: 'Why don't you take a little break and relax?'

Anyone can master amigurumi, and there are no limits to what you can create. Grab some yarn and crochet hooks, get comfortable by the fire, and start making your own little world.

Tools and Materials

Basic Crochet Kit

Crochet hooks come in a great variety of materials, from wooden and plastic to chunky steel and even ivory. All come in different shapes and sizes. Different countries have different sizing systems – which can be confusing – so always double-check your hook against the conversion charts. Check also that you are using the correct size hook as indicated in the pattern. All of the patterns in this book use a size 4 crochet hook. However, remember that experimenting with various weights and types of yarn will require different-sized hooks; the important thing is to use a hook that will give a nice tight crochet with the selected yarn.

Knitter's pins with large heads (useful for pinning shapes).

Blunt-ended needle for sewing up.

Split stitch markers for marking the beginnings of rounds.

Tape measure

Sharp scissors

Tweezers to help with stuffing.

Embroidery needle for embroidering faces and details.

Embroidery thread

Craft wire or pipe cleaners for parts that need more shaping.

Well-spun yarns are the best to achieve neat, tidy work.

Fine crochet cotton (lace) thread has a firm texture, that is good for beaks. Its thickness is given in numbers, i.e., 5, 10, and so on. The higher the number, the finer the thread.

4-ply yarn is good in general, especially for making smaller creatures.

DK yarn is good for making large monsters, but make sure the crochet is as tight as possible so the stuffing can't be seen. You can achieve different results in amigurumi depending on what size or type of yarn you use, even when you are working on the same pattern. The thicker the yarn, the bigger your amigurumi will be!

Mohair is good for making your monsters look extra scary-cute and fluffy.

Plastic eyes and noses for facial adornments.

Felt

Scraps of yarn to use as scarves or patches to dress up the amigurumi.

Cotton wadding is the most commonly used material for stuffing amigurumi creatures, but you could also use scraps of yarn for the really tiny monsters.

Techniques

Reading Patterns

If this is the first time that you have used crochet patterns, you might feel like you are learning a new language. However, you will soon begin to recognize the abbreviations used in crochet. The abbreviations make patterns shorter and easier to follow.

Let's learn the new crochet language.

Crochet Abbreviations

alt	alternate
approx	approximately
beg	begin/beginning
bet	between
ch	chain stitch
cm	centimetre(s)
col	colour
cont	continue
dc	double crochet
dc2tog	double crochet 2 stitches together
dtr	double treble crochet
dec	decrease/decreasing/decreases
foll	follow/follows/following
htr	half treble crochet
inc	increase/increases/increasing
mm	millimetre
rep	repeat(s)
sc	single crochet
sk	skip/miss
ss	slip stitch
st(s)	stitch(es)
tog	together
tr	treble
yoh	yarn over hook
*	repeat that step

Now, it's time to step into the hook-sizing world.

Both the metric and UK sizes can appear on the packaging of hooks. It is useful to know how to convert sizes. Here is the converter for hook sizes.

METRIC	OLD UK
2.5 mm	12
3 mm	11
3.25 mm	10
3.5 mm	9
4 mm	8
4.25 mm	8
5 mm	6
5.5 mm	5
6 mm	4
7 mm	2
8 mm	0
9 mm	00
10 mm	000
15 mm	000

How to read a Japanese crochet chart
On the Japanese chart, each stitch is shown as follows:

- **Magic ring:** tiny circle in the middle of circular chart   O
- **Double crochet:** cross   X
- **Treble crochet:** T symbol   T
- **Chain stitch:** tiny oval   o
- **Arrow pointing toward the centre of the diagram:** increasing   >
- **Arrow pointing away from the centre of the diagram:** decreasing   <
- **Slip stitch:** black oval   ●

Follow the chart from the centre to the outside, then move to the non-circular part of the chart, if there is one shown above the circular part. Always follow the chart anti-clockwise.

Crochet Techniques

Crochet is all about mixing really simple techniques with more elaborate flourishes. Once you get the hang of making chains, you are ready to progress to a variety of fancy stitches.

Holding the hook and yarn

Learning how to hold the hook and yarn correctly is the first step to crochet. Most people hold the hook and yarn as they would a pencil or a knife, but you should experiment to find the most comfortable way for you.

Mastering the slipknot

Making a slipknot is the first step in any project. Master the slipknot technique, and you are on your way to super crochet!

Make a loop in the yarn. With your hook, catch the ball end of the yarn and draw it through the loop. Pull firmly on the yarn and hook to tighten the knot and create your first loop.

Making a chain

1. Before making a chain, you need to place the slipknot on a hook. To make a chain, hold the tail end of the yarn with the left hand and bring the yarn over the hook by passing the hook in front of the yarn, under and around it.

2. Keeping the tension in the yarn taut, draw the hook and yarn through the loop.

3. Pull the yarn, hook it through the hole, and begin again, ensuring that the stitches are fairly loose. Repeat to make the number of chains required. As the chain lengthens, keep hold of the bottom edge to maintain the tension.

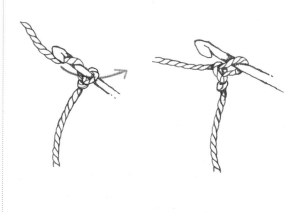

How to count a chain

To count the stitches, use the right side of the chain, or the side that has more visible and less twisted 'V' shapes, as shown. Do not count the original slip stitch, but count each 'V' as one chain.

Making a slip stitch (ss)

A slip stitch is used to join one stitch to another or a stitch to another point, as in joining a circle, and is usually made by picking up two strands of a stitch. However, where it is worked into the starting chain, only pick up the back loop.

1. Insert the hook into the back loop of the next stitch and pass yarn over hook (yoh), as in the chain stitch.

2. Draw yarn through both loops of stitch and repeat.

The magic ring: working in the round

There are two ways to start circular crochet. One is with a chain and another is with a loop. A loop, or magic ring, is the more usual way to make amigurumi. This way of working in the round ensures that there is no hole in the middle of the work, as there is with a chain ring, because the central hole is adjustable and can be pulled tightly closed.

Let's make a magic ring

This will be the first round of your amigurumi, so you need to master it!

1. Make a loop by wrapping the yarn twice onto your forefinger, with the tail end of the yarn on the right, the ball end on the left.

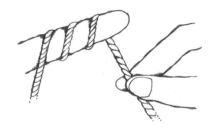

2. Pull the ball end through the loop (steady your work with your hand).

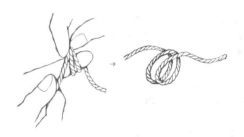

3. Make one chain (ch) through the loop on the hook you have drawn through to steady the round.

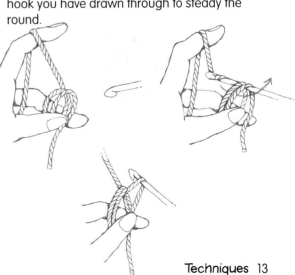

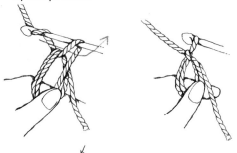

4. Work as many double crochet (dc), or whatever stitch you are using, into the loop as is required by the pattern.

5. Pull the last stitch out long enough so that it won't come undone. Find out which loop will be tightened first by pulling one of the loops.

6. Pull this loop as tight as you can.

7. Pull the tail end of the yarn to tighten up the whole loop. Now you have no hole in the middle of the first round.

Completing the magic ring: first round

Insert the hook into the first stitch of a magic ring and pull the yarn through all the way.

This is called 'slip stitch' (ss).

Start the second round

To crochet a flat circle, you need to keep working in the round with increasing stitches.

1. Make one chain (ch). Insert the hook into the first stitch of a circle, and put the yarn over the hook (yoh) and then draw the yarn through the loop. This is called double crochet (dc). In amigurumi, this is the technique you will use the most.

2. Add one more dc into the same stitch. This is called increasing (inc).

Repeat 1 and 2 into every stitch and you will finish the second round with twice the number of stitches.

On the second round, increase in alternate stitches.

Third round: 1 dc into each of the next 2 stitches, 2 dc into the next one. Repeat.

Fourth round: 1 dc into each of the next 3 stitches, 2 dc into the next one. Repeat.

The more rounds you go, the more stitches you need to make between increases.

Making a chain ring

1. Work a chain as long as required by the pattern.

2. Join the last chain to the first with a slip stitch (ss). Begin the first round by working into each chain stitch.

Variety of stitches

Double crochet (dc): The main stitch used for amigurumi

1. Insert the hook, front to back, into the next stitch. Yoh.

2. Draw through one loop to front; there should be two loops on the hook. Yoh.

3. Draw through both loops to complete double crochet.

Treble crochet (tr)

This makes a more open fabric as the stitches are taller.

1. Wrap the yarn over the hook (yoh) from back to front. Insert the hook into the next stitch, from front to back. Yoh again and draw through the stitch.

2. There should be three loops on the hook. Yoh and pull through two loops. Yoh and draw through first two.

3. There should be two loops on the hook. Yoh. Pull through the remaining two loops. Yoh and draw through last two to complete.

Half-treble (htr)

The half-treble is simply that: half of a treble crochet. Therefore, the stitch is slightly shorter than treble crochet. In step 2 of treble, pull through all the remaining loops in one movement.

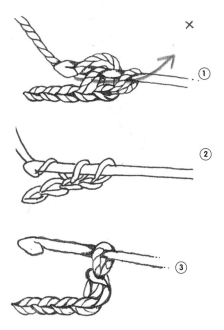

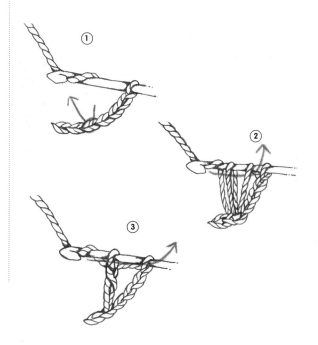

Fastening Off

If you want your little monster to be perfect, fastening off is the most important step – and also the most nerve-racking. The key to success in every amigurumi project is perfect assembly.

Here are some useful things to remember:

When you fasten off the ends of the arms and legs, leave a long tail for sewing the pieces together. Do not weave this end in.

Connect two pieces by taking stitches alternately from each piece and fastening them securely.

Fastening off

1. After fastening off the last stitch, snip off the yarn from the ball, leaving a couple of centimetres to weave in.

2. Draw through the last loop, pulling tightly to fasten.

Weaving in ends

1. Use the hook to draw the yarn through at least five stitches, weaving the yarn over and under as you go to secure the yarn and ensure it does not work free.

2. Snip off the excess yarn.

When fastening off the creature, attach all pieces, leaving openings for stuffing where appropriate. Stuff firmly, sew up gaps and embroider features as shown in the illustrations.

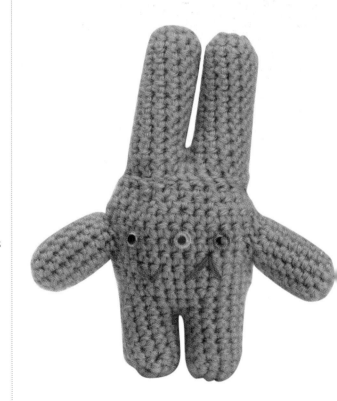

Designing Your Own Monsters

There are no strict rules in crochet. As soon as you grab your crochet hook and get the hang of it, it's as easy as drawing pictures! In the following section, you'll learn the process for creating your very own, very scary-cute amigurumi. However, keep in mind that you don't have to follow this method exactly. Once you start making your own monsters, you're sure to discover your own techniques.

Developing your design

Any weird creatures you can think of can turn into amigurumi.

You can develop your designs from anything you see in the world around you. Try looking through children's picture books for animals, plants, and other creatures that could be turned into your very first little monsters.

Another great place to source inspiration is the encyclopedia. From A to Z, it's just filled with endless design ideas.

Once you have an idea, play around with various shapes that will then become the base or body of the monster. Try experimenting with all sorts of unusual shapes, like spheres, eggs, cubes, tubes, and so on.

Some of your creations might have extremely long legs, while others might have more (or less) than two eyes. Don't be afraid to really express your creativity and reignite your childhood imagination!

Sketching

Start by making a rough sketch (see the opposite page for some examples). Don't worry about these first sketches being in full colour, or even very neat, as they are just ideas to get you started. The samples shown here are drawn with pencil, and only partially filled in with coloured pencil.

Choosing materials

Amigurumi means 'knitted or crocheted doll', but this doesn't mean that all you can use to create your monsters is a ball of wool.

The choice of materials is endless. By playing with a variety of materials, you'll discover interesting differences in textures.

Yarn is a basic material and always a good one to start with. However, there is even a huge variety in the types of yarns.

Shaping your monster

This section will show you how to create the basic shapes for your monsters. Once you've mastered this, you can change the shapes to create all kinds of different creatures!

Take a look at the monster below.

This monster is made up of 4 different shapes (labelled A, B, C, and D).

A: Ball/sphere

Keep increasing stitches until the disc is the size of sphere you want to make. Carry on for a couple of rounds without changing, and then start decreasing.

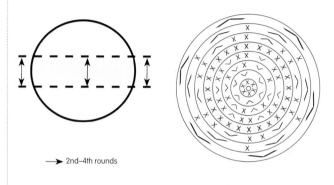

→ 2nd–4th rounds

B: Body

For the basic body shape, divide the work into 3 sections to achieve a longish eggplant-looking shape.

The number of rounds for each part (coloured yellow, pink and green) varies depending on how long the shape needs to be.

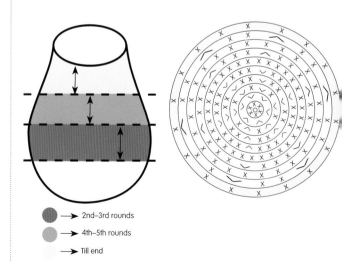

→ 2nd–3rd rounds

→ 4th–5th rounds

→ Till end

C: Ears or horns

This part is really simple. Just make a disc in the size you want, then continue with dc until the section is the length you require.

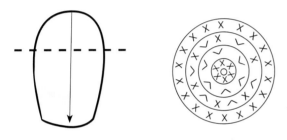

→ Keep dc without changing number of stitches

D: Round legs

To make the legs, use the same method as in C, but make the shapes shorter.

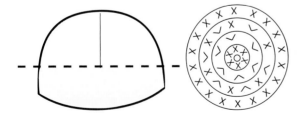

→ Same as C but shorter

For a nice round shape, use the number of stitches detailed in the pattern.

Then, make a couple of rounds without changing the number of stitches until the end.

Of course, the number of stitches used here is only a suggestion. You can alter the patterns for the shape you want to make.

Once you get the gist of this technique, it's easy to create all kinds of new shapes. Have fun!

Chapter 1

Adorable
Aliens

Many-heads Monster

Nothing gets past this starship trooper. There's nowhere to hide from the multi-eyed Many-heads Monster. So it's warp-speed ahead and set phasers to stun if you're going to escape his scary-cute clutches.

Materials

HOOK SIZE: 4mm

YARN: Pink (DK) Green (DK) Purple (DK)
        Baby Blue (DK)

EYES: 4mm

Head (need 3)

Make each head a slightly different length and a different colour.

Use baby blue, green or purple yarn.

Make a loop with the tail end of the yarn on the right, keeping the ball end on the left.

Pull the ball end through the loop. Make one ch through the loop on the hook you have drawn through to steady the circle. 6dc into the circle and join to the first DK with ss to complete.

1st round: 2dc into each of 6dc. (12sts)

2nd round: *1dc. 2dc into next dc. *6 times. (18sts)

1dc into all sts for 8 rounds.

Change to pink yarn, then dc all for another 2 rounds.

Fasten off.

Repeat twice so you end up with 3 heads.

Body

Use pink yarn.

Start the same way as you did for the head, 6dc in a circle.

1st round: 2dc into each of 6dc. (12sts)

2nd round: *1dc. 2dc into next dc. *6 times. (18sts)

3rd round: *1dc into each of next 2dc, 2dc into next dc. *6 times. (24sts)

4th round: *1dc into each of next 3dc, 2dc into next dc.*6 times. (30sts)

5th–7th round: 1dc into all sts. (30sts)

8th round: *1dc into each of 3dc. Skip 1, 1dc. *6 times. (24sts)

9th round: *1dc into each of 2dc. Skip 1, 1dc. *6 times. (18sts)

10th round: *1dc, skip 1, 1dc. *6 times. (12sts)

11th round: 1dc into every alternate st. (6sts)

Stuff the body, then fasten off.

Legs (need 2)

Use the pink yarn and start the same way as you did for the head.

1st round: 2dc into each of 6dc. (12sts)

Keep working in dc for 1½in (4cm).

Fasten off.

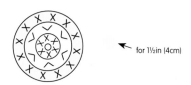

for 1½in (4cm)

Finishing

Stuff all parts and sew them onto the body.

Trumpet Thing

This crazy creature from beyond the stars has crashed his spaceship on Earth – he's armed and could be dangerous. Watch out for Trumpet Thing's wildly waving suckers. Will he use them to drain your life force, or just tickle your fancy?

Materials

HOOK SIZE: 4mm

YARN: Green (DK) Purple (DK) Orange (DK)

EYES: 4mm

Body

Use green yarn. Make a loop with the tail end of the yarn on the right, keeping the ball end on the left.

Pull the ball end through the loop. Make one ch through the loop on the hook you have drawn through to steady the circle. 6dc into the circle and join to the first DK with ss to complete.

1st round: 2dc into each of 6dc. (12sts)

2nd round: *1dc. 2dc into next dc. *6 times. (18sts)

3rd round: *1dc into each of next 2dc, 2dc into next dc. *6 times. (24sts)

4th–6th round: *1dc into all sts.

7th round: *1dc into next 6dc, skip 1, 1dc. *3 times. (21sts)

8th round: 1dc into all dc.

9th round: *1dc into next 5dc, skip 1, 1dc. *3 times. (18sts)

10th round: 1dc into all sts.

11th round: *1dc into next 4dc, skip 1, 1dc. *3 times. (15sts)

12th round: 1dc into all dc.

13th round: *1dc into next 3dc. Skip 1, 1dc. *3 times. (12sts)

14th round: *1dc, skip 1. *Repeat for one round.

Fasten off.

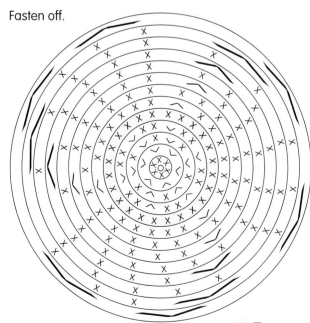

4th–6th round

Ears (need 2)

Using the orange yarn, start in the same 6dc-into-a-circle way.

1dc into each 6dc for 1½in (4cm). Actually, you can make it as long as you want.

Next round: 2dc into all sts.

Next round: *1dc, 2dc into the next dc. *6 times. (18sts)

Next round: *1dc into next 2dc, 2dc to next dc. *6 times. (24sts)

Fasten off.

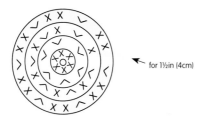

for 1½in (4cm)

Trumpet nose

Using purple yarn, repeat the pattern for the ears to create the nose.

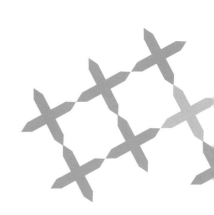

Special ET

Take me to your leader! Special ET has just landed, and he's ready for a close encounter of the scary kind. Will you run screaming from this alien life-form, or can you make friends with a furry thing from outer space?

Materials

HOOK SIZE: 4mm

YARN: Turquoise (DK) Orange (DK) Pink (DK)

EYES: 9mm

Head (2 parts joined together)

Use pink yarn.

(Section A)

Make a loop with the tail end of the yarn on the right, keeping the ball end on the left.

Pull the ball end through the loop. Make one ch through the loop on the hook you have drawn through to steady the circle. 6dc into the circle and join to the first DK with ss to complete.

1st round: 2dc into each of 6dc. (12sts)

2nd–3rd round: 1dc into all sts. (12sts)

4th round: *1dc into each of next 4sts, skip 1, 1dc. *Twice. (10sts)

5th–9th round: 1dc into all sts. (10sts)

Fasten off.

(Section B)

Use the same method as for Section A.

1st round: 2dc into each of 6dc. (12sts)

2nd–3rd round: 1dc into all sts. (12sts)

4th round: *1dc into each of next 4sts, skip 1, 1dc. *Twice. (10sts)

5th–6th round: 1dc into all sts. (10sts)

Fasten off.

Stuff each section and sew section B onto A. (See diagram below).

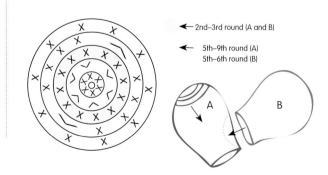

← 2nd–3rd round (A and B)

← 5th–9th round (A)
5th–6th round (B)

A   B

Body

Use turquoise yarn.

Start with the same 6dc-in-a-circle method.

1st round: 2dc into each of 6dc. (12sts)

2nd round: *1dc. 2dc into next dc. *6 times. (18sts)

3rd round: *1dc into each of next 2dc, 2dc into next dc. *6 times. (24sts)

4th round: *1dc into each of next 3dc, 2dc into next dc.*6 times. (30sts)

5th–7th round: 1dc into all sts. (30sts)

8th round: *1dc into each of 8dc. Skip 1, 1dc. *3 times. (27sts)

9th round: 1dc into all sts. (27sts)

10th round: *1dc into each of next 7dc, skip 1, 1dc. *3 times. (24sts)

11th round: 1dc into all sts. (24sts)

12th round: *1dc into each of next 6dc, skip 1, 1dc. *3 times. (21sts)

13th round: 1dc into all sts. (21sts)

14th round: *1dc into each of next 6dc, skip 1, 1dc. *3 times. (18sts)

15th–18th round: 1dc into all sts. (18sts)

19th–20th round: Change the yarn to pink to match to the head. 1dc into all. (18sts)

Fasten off.

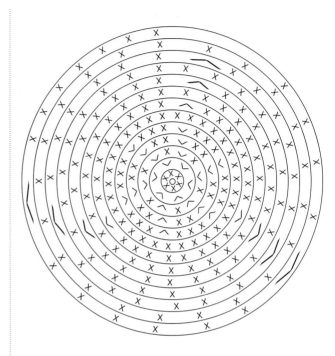

Legs (need 2)

Use orange yarn.

Start in the same way as for all the other parts (a circle with 6dc).

1st round: *1dc into next dc, 2dc into next. *3 times. (9sts)

2nd–4th round: 1dc into all sts. (9sts)

5th round: 1dc into all, skipping every alternate dc. (6sts)

Stuff the leg and fasten off.

Finishing (see illustration)

Stuff all parts.

Sew the head parts onto the body.

Sew the legs onto the bottom of the body.

← 2nd–4th round

Pink Attack

The mother ship has landed! Beware the two-faced terror that is Pink Attack – does she come in peace or ready for battle? You might have to fight this scary extraterrestrial mite, but a cosmic cuddle may be enough to prevent all-out intergalactic war.

Materials

HOOK SIZE: 4mm

YARN: Pink (DK)
     Scrap of red yarn (4-ply)

EYES: 6mm

Legs (need 2)

Start with the pink yarn.

Make a loop with the tail end of the yarn on the right, keeping the ball end on the left.

Pull the ball end through the loop. Make one ch through the loop on the hook you have drawn through to steady the circle. 6dc into the circle and join to the first DK with ss to complete.

1st round: 2dc into each of 6dc. (12sts)

2nd round: *1dc. 2dc into next dc. *6 times. (18sts)

3rd round: *1dc into each of next 2dc, 2dc into next dc. *6 times. (24sts)

4th–8th round: 1dc into all sts. (24sts)

Join 2 tubes (legs) together by making a couple of stitches together to secure. (See diagram on p.40.)

Pick up 24sts from top of the legs.

Body

1dc into each dc for 2 rounds with pink yarn.

Next round: *1dc into each of next 3dc, 2dc into next dc. *6 times. (30sts)

1dc into each dc for 3 rounds.

Next round: *1dc into each of next 3dc, skip 1, 1dc *6 times. (24sts)

1dc into all sts for next 2 rounds. (24sts)

Fasten off.

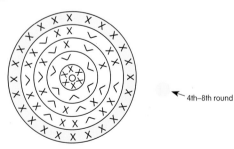

4th–8th round

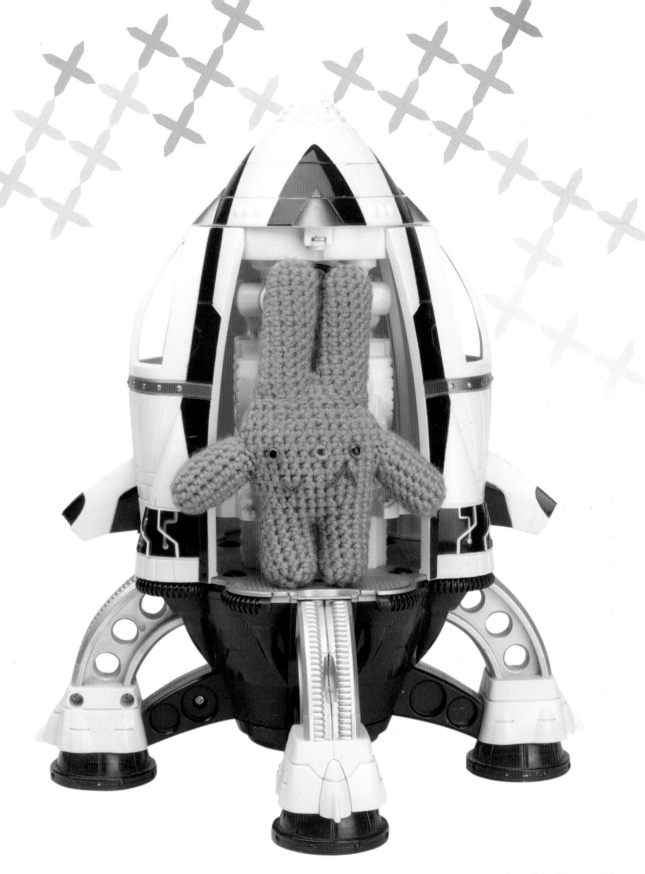

Ears

For the ears, use exactly the same pattern as for the legs, but make them slightly longer.

Arms (need 2)

Make the arms using the same pattern as the one for the legs and ears.

However, you do not need to join them together as you do the legs.

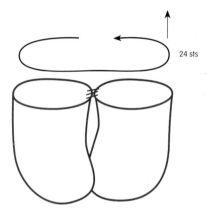

24 sts

The same pattern is used for the legs and arms.
You need 2 of each.

Finishing

Stuff all parts and sew them onto the main body.

With a scrap of red yarn, embroider on a mouth. Her expression can reflect the mood you're in!

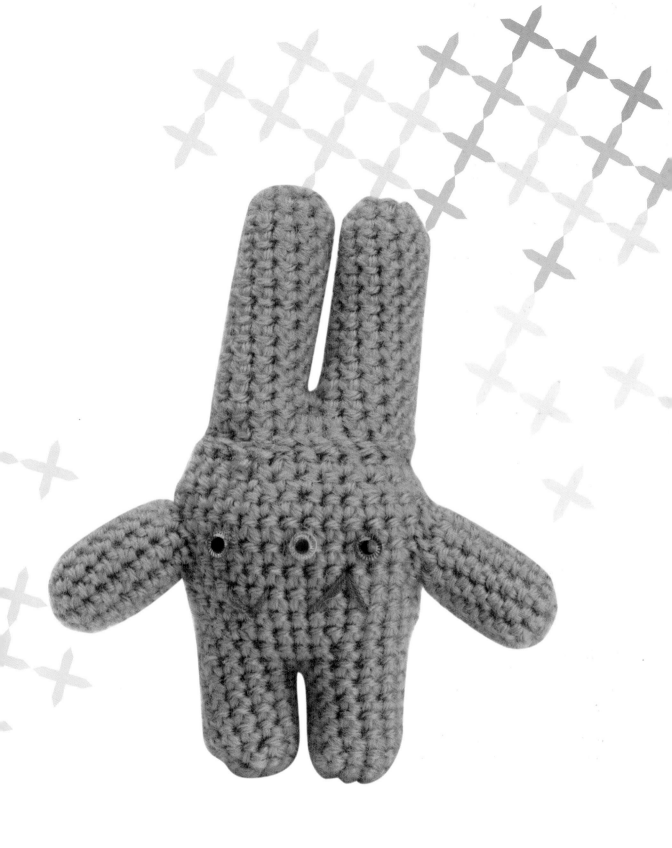

Cheeky Face

Long ago, in a galaxy far, far away, an alien being emerged from its bubble-pod and Cheeky Face was born. Now she's left her home planet and travelled across time and space to capture earthlings – by surprise! – and steal their hearts.

Materials

HOOK SIZE: 4mm

YARN: Green (DK) Pink (DK) Beige (DK)

EYES: 9mm

Horns (need 2)

Use green yarn. Make a loop with the tail end of the yarn on the right, keeping the ball end on the left.

Pull the ball end through the loop. Make one ch through the loop on the hook you have drawn through to steady the circle. 6dc into the circle and join to the first DK with ss to complete.

1st round: 2dc into each of 6dc. (12sts)

1dc into all sts for 6 rounds, then fasten off.

To make the second horn, use the pink yarn and repeat these instructions.

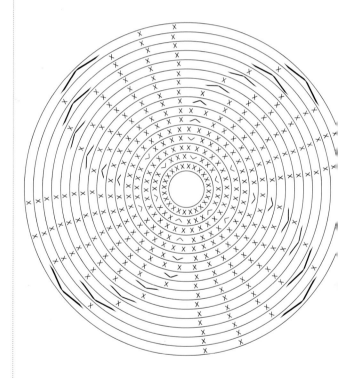

Body

Join 2 tubes (horns) with a couple of stitches between them. (See illustration.)

Pick up 24 stitches around the two joined horns.

Next round: *1dc into next 3dc. 2dc into the next dc. *6 times. (30sts)

Next round: 1dc into all dc for next 2 rounds. (30sts)

Next round: *1dc into next 4dc, 2dc into the next dc. *6 times. (36sts)

Next round: *1dc into all sts for 2 rounds in pink yarn, then change the yarn back to green and 1dc into all sts for another 5dc.

Next round: *1dc into next 7dc, skip 1, 1dc into next dc.*4 times. (32sts)

Next round: *1dc into all dc.

Next round: *1dc into next 6dc, skip 1, 1dc into next dc.*4 times. (28sts)

Next round: 1dc into all sts. (28sts)

Next round: *1dc into next 5dc, skip 1, 1dc into next dc.*4 times. (24sts)

Next round: 1dc into all sts. (24sts)

Next round: *1dc into next 4dc, skip 1, 1dc. *4 times. (20sts)

Next round: 1dc into all dc.

Next round: *1dc into next 3dc, skip 1, 1dc. *4 times. (16sts)

Next round: 1dc into all dc.

Next round: *1dc into next 2dc, skip 1, 1dc. *4 times. (12sts)

Next round: *1dc, skip 1. *6 times. (6sts)

Fasten off.

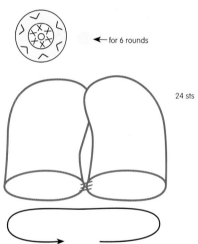

← for 6 rounds

24 sts

Face

With beige yarn, make a loop with the tail end of the yarn on the right, keeping the ball end on the left.

Pull the ball end through the loop. Make one ch through the loop on the hook you have drawn through to steady the circle. 6dc into the circle and join to the first DK with ss to complete.

1st round: 2dc into each of 6dc. (12sts)

2nd round: *1dc. 2dc into next dc. *6 times. (18sts)

3rd round: *1dc into each of next 2dc, 2dc into next dc. *6 times. (24sts)

Fasten off.

Finishing

Stuff the body.

Stitch the face disc onto the body.

Chapter 2
MONSTERS
from the
DEEP

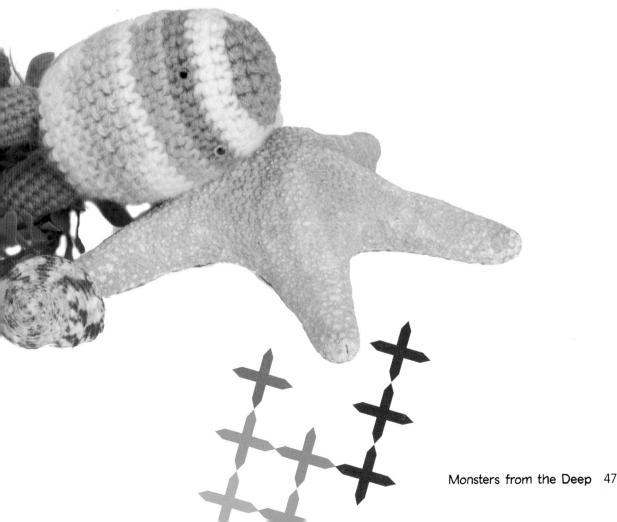

Pretty Sea Flower

This innocent-looking creature lurks in rock pools, close to the shore. But don't be taken in by Pretty Sea Flower's charms. That fluffy pink topknot hides a vicious sting – she'll catch you unawares and then go in for the kill.

Materials

HOOK SIZE: 4mm

YARN: Blue mohair   Green mohair   Purple mohair
Pink yarn for topknot

EYES: 9mm

Head

Use blue yarn. Make a loop with the tail end of the yarn on the right, keeping the ball end on the left.

Pull the ball end through the loop. Make one ch through the loop on the hook you have drawn through to steady the circle. 6dc into the circle and join to the first DK with ss to complete.

1st round: 2dc into each of 6dc. (12sts)

2nd round: *1dc. 2dc into next dc. *6 times. (18sts)

3rd round: *1dc into each of next 2dc, 2dc into next dc. *6 times. (24sts)

4th round: *1dc into each of next 3dc, 2dc into next dc.*6 times. (30sts)

5th–8th round: 1dc into all sts. (30sts)

9th round: *1dc into next 8dc, skip 1, 1dc. *3 times. (27sts)

10th round: 1dc into all sts.

11th round: *1dc into next 7dc, skip 1, 1dc. *3 times. (24sts)

12th–14th round: 1dc into all sts.

Change to green yarn.

15th round: *1dc, 1htr, 3tr, 1htr, 1dc into the same dc. Skip 1. *Repeat all the way around. (This will make a curly, frilled effect.)

16th round: Pick up the bar from one of the dc you made on the previous round and repeat for another round. The stitches can be as random as you want them to be. Experiment with the number of dc and tr to see how the frill will look.

Fasten off.

Use purple yarn. Crochet a disc to close the bottom of head.

Make a loop with the tail end of the yarn on the right, keeping the ball end on the left.

Pull the ball end through the loop. Make one ch through the loop on the hook you have drawn through to steady the circle. 6dc into the circle and join to the first DK with ss to complete.

1st round: 2dc into each of 6dc. (12sts)

2nd round: *1dc. 2dc into next dc. *6 times. (18sts)

Fasten off.

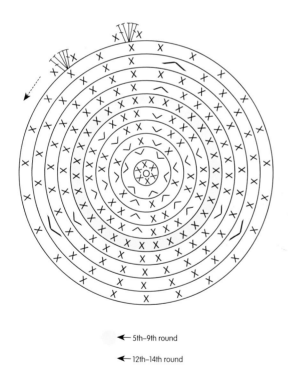

← 5th–9th round

← 12th–14th round

Topknot

Use pink yarn.

1st round: 2dc into each of 6dc. (12sts)

2nd round: 1dc into all sts.

3rd round: 1dc into all sts.

Fasten off.

Finishing

Stuff the body and close it by stitching the crochet disc (see illustration below) on the bottom.

Scary Squid

Within the abyss dwell the worst terrors of the deep. Most fearsome of all is Scary Squid, sleeping in his lair at the bottom of the ocean. Don't wake this cute kraken or you might fall prey to a scary squirt of ink.

Materials

HOOK SIZE: 4mm

YARN: Yellow (DK) Pink (DK) Blue (DK)

EYES: 9mm

Head-Body

Use yellow yarn. Make a loop with the tail end of the yarn on the right, keeping the ball end on the left.

Pull the ball end through the loop. Make one ch through the loop on the hook you have drawn through to steady the circle. 6dc into the circle and join to the first DK with ss to complete.

1st round: 2dc into each of 6dc. (12sts)

2nd round: *1dc. 2dc into next dc. *6 times. (18sts)

3rd–11th round: 1dc into all sts.

(From here, work in rows.)

Make 3 sections for the legs.

1st row: 1dc into the first of each 6dc on the round, then turn.

2nd–8th row: 1dc into all sts. Then make 1ch to turn and start the new row.

9th row: 2dc together, 1dc to next 2dc, 2dc together. (4sts)

10th row: 2dc together and another 2dc together. (2sts)

Fasten off.

Repeat instructions to make another 2 legs.

Start by picking 6sts and then follow the pattern.

Using pink yarn, pick up all sts around the 3 leg sections with dc.

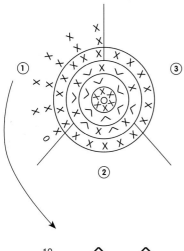

```
10        ∧       ∧
9      ∧  X   X   ∧
8    0 X  X   X   X  X
7    X X  X   X   X  0
6    0 X  X   X   X  X
5    X X  X   X   X  0
4    0 X  X   X   X  X
3    X X  X   X   X  0
2    0 X  X   X   X  X
1    X X  X   X   X  X
       0  0  0  0  0  0
```

Change to blue yarn.

1dc into all sts for 2 rounds.

*1dc into each of next 2dc, skip 1, 1dc. *Repeat all the way around.

Next round: *1dc, skip 1, 1dc. *Repeat all the way around.

Next round: *1dc, skip 1. *Repeat all the way around.

Repeat 1dc, skip 1, until the hole in the middle is closed.

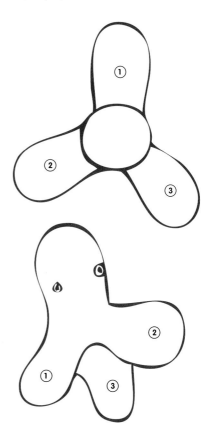

Something Fishy

If you feel like going for a dip, watch out! Just beneath the surface of the silvery sea, you'll find Something Fishy. Could this marine menace eat you up with one snap of his terrible jaws?
Or is he just a furry, fishy fraud?

Materials

HOOK SIZE: 4mm

YARN: Green (DK) Bright Orange (DK) Pink (DK)

(Or use any colour you like!)

EYES: 4mm

Body

Use green yarn to start, then change the colour every 3 rounds. However, this is only a suggestion and you can experiment with your coloured stripes.

Make a loop with the tail end of the yarn on the right, keeping the ball end on the left.

Pull the ball end through the loop. Make one ch through the loop on the hook you have drawn through to steady the circle. 6dc into the circle and join to the first DK with ss to complete.

1st round: 2dc into each of 6dc. (12sts)

2nd round: *1dc. 2dc into next dc. *6 times. (18sts)

3rd round: *1dc into each of next 2dc, 2dc into next dc. *6 times. (24sts)

4th round: *1dc into each of next 3dc, 2dc into next dc.*6 times. (30sts)

5th–8th round: 1dc into all sts. (30sts)

9th round: *1dc into each of next 8dc, skip 1, 1dc. *3 times. (27sts)

10th round: 1dc into all sts. (27sts)

11th round: *1dc into each of next 7dc, skip 1, 1dc. *3 times. (24sts)

12th round: 1dc into all sts. (24sts)

13th round: *1dc into each of next 4sts, skip 1, 1dc. *4 times. (20sts)

14th round: 1dc into all sts. (20sts)

15th round: *1dc into each of next 3sts, skip 1, 1dc. *4 times. (16sts)

16th round: *1dc into each of next 2sts, skip 1, 1dc. *4 times. (12sts)

17th round: 1dc into every alternate st. (6sts)

Stuff the body, then fasten off.

Body

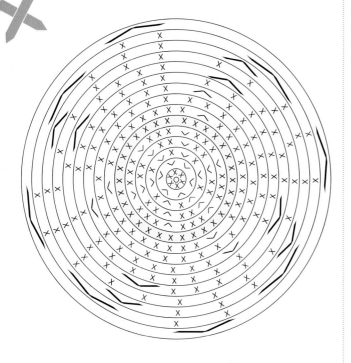

← 5th–8th round

Tail fins (need 2)

Use green yarn.

Start in the same way as you did for the body, making a circle with 6dc.

1st round: 2dc into each of 6dc. (12sts)

Continue to dc for 1¼in (3cm).

Fasten off.

Finishing

Stuff the fins and sew them onto the body.

Crazy Beast

Crazy Beast is one mixed-up mutant monster. Part crab, part cockle, she scuttles along the sea bed, waiting to pounce on unsuspecting paddlers. Why not risk a toe and see if you can coax this cute crustacean out of her shell?

Materials

HOOK SIZE: 4mm

YARN: Green (DK) Baby Blue (DK) Blue (DK)
      Scraps of orange yarn and pink yarn.

EYES: 9mm

Head

Use green yarn.

Make a loop with the tail end of the yarn on the right, keeping the ball end on the left.

Pull the ball end through the loop. Make one ch through the loop on the hook you have drawn through to steady the circle. 6dc into the circle and join to the first DK with ss to complete.

1st round: 2dc into each of 6dc. (12sts)

2nd round: *1dc, 2dc into next dc. *6 times. (18sts)

3rd round: *1dc into each of next 2dc, 2dc into next dc. *6 times. (24sts)

4th round: *1dc into each of next 3dc, 2dc into next dc. *6 times. (30sts)

5th round: *1dc into each of next 4dc, 2dc into next dc.*6 times. (36sts)

Continue to dc for 10 rounds.

Fasten off.

for 10 rounds

Disc to close the bottom of head

Use baby blue yarn.

Start in the same way as you did to make the head.

1st round: 2dc into each of 6dc. (12sts)

2nd round: *1dc. 2dc into next dc. *6 times. (18sts)

3rd round: *1dc into each of next 2dc, 2dc into next dc. *6 times. (24sts)

4th round: *1dc into each of next 3dc, 2dc into next dc. *6 times. (30sts)

5th round: *1dc into each of next 4dc, 2dc into next dc.*6 times. (36sts)

Fasten off.

Legs (need 2)

Use blue yarn.

Start in the same way, making a circle with 6dc, to make the body.

1st round: 2dc into each of 6dc. (12sts)

Continue to dc for 1¼in (3cm).

Fasten off.

Finishing

Stuff the body and close it with the crochet disc.

Sew the legs onto the body.

With scraps of yarn, embroider on a little head fringe and a mouth.

Green Stinger

If you thought it was safe to go back in the water, think again! Green Stinger is there, lying in wait beneath the waves. With terrifying tentacles and razor-sharp teeth, this scary sea-beast is a real monster of the deep.

Materials

HOOK SIZE: 4mm

YARN: Green (DK)
        White felt for mouth

EYES: 10mm

Legs (need 3)

Use green yarn.

Make a loop with the tail end of the yarn on the right, keeping the ball end on the left.

Pull the ball end through the loop. Make one ch through the loop on the hook you have drawn through to steady the circle. 6dc into the circle and join to the first DK with ss to complete.

1st round: 2dc into each of 6dc. (12sts)

2nd–9th round: 1dc into all sts.

Fasten off.

Make 2 more legs (you need 3 in total).

Join tubes (legs) together with a couple of stitches to secure. (See illustration.)

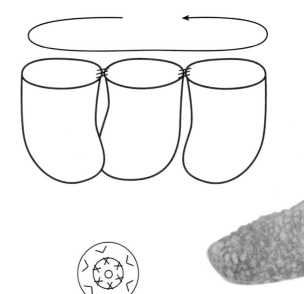

2nd–9th rounds

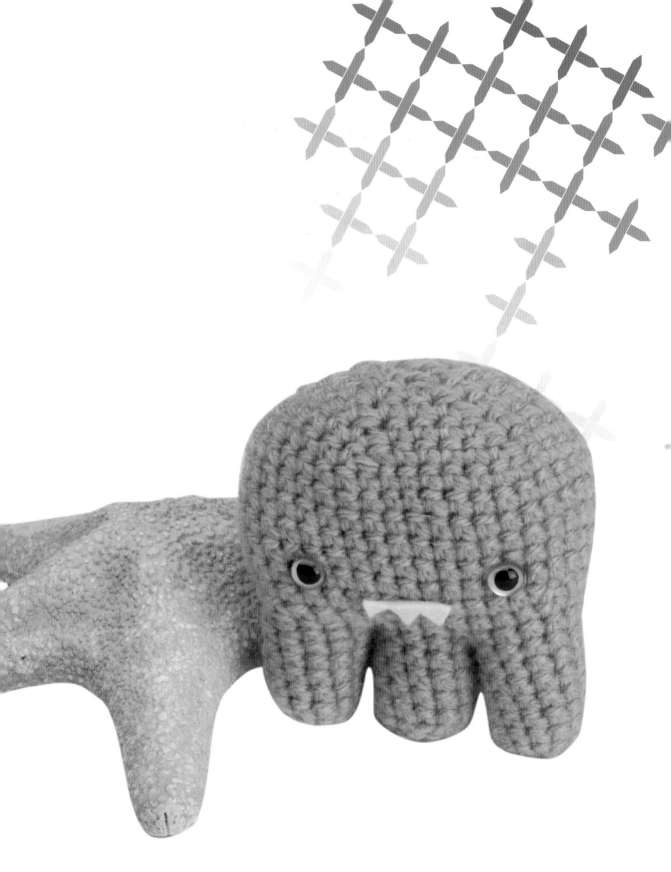

Body

Pick up 30 sts from top of the legs.

1dc into each dc for 2 rounds.

Next round: *1dc into each of next 4dc, 2dc into next dc. *6 times. (36sts)

Next round: 1dc into each dc for 3 rounds.

Next round: *1dc into each of next 4dc, skip 1, 1dc. *6 times. (30sts)

Next round: *1dc into each of next 3dc, skip 1, 1dc. *6 times. (24sts)

Next round: *1dc into each of next 2dc, skip 1, 1 dc. *6 times. (18sts)

Next round: *1dc, skip 1, 1dc. *6 times. (12sts)

Stuff the body, then 1dc into every alternate dc on the last round. (6sts)

Fasten off.

Cut out teeth from white felt and attach to the monster.

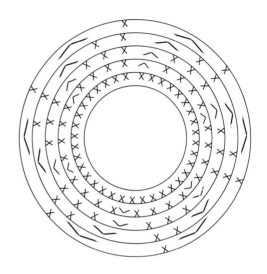

Chapter 3
Little Horrors

Baby Vampire

In the deepest, darkest night, Baby Vampire emerges from his scary-cute coffin to look for fresh victims: He wants to suck your blood! You'll have to eat a lot of garlic if you want to stop this fanged fiend from worming his way into your heart.

Materials

HOOK SIZE: 4mm

YARN: Brown (DK) Orange (DK) Yellow (DK)
Scraps of white felt and red yarn

EYES: 9mm

Body

Use brown yarn.

Make a loop with the tail end of the yarn on the right, keeping the ball end on the left.

Pull the ball end through the loop. Make one ch through the loop on the hook you have drawn through to steady the circle. 6dc into the circle and join to the first DK with ss to complete.

1st round: 2dc into each of 6dc. (12sts)

2nd round: *1dc. 2dc into next dc. *6 times. (18sts)

3rd round: *1dc into each of next 2dc, 2dc into next dc. *6 times. (24sts)

4th round: *1dc into each of next 3dc, 2dc into next dc. *6 times. (30sts)

5th round: *1dc into each of next 4dc, 2dc into next dc.*6 times. (36sts)

6th–10th round: 1dc into all sts.

11th round: *1dc into each of next 4dc, skip 1, 1dc. *6 times. (30sts)

12th–13th round: 1dc into all sts.

14th round: *1dc into each of next 3dc, skip 1, 1dc. *6 times. (24sts)

15th-16th round: 1dc into all sts.

17th round: *1dc into each of next 2dc, skip 1, 1dc. *6 times. (18sts)

18th round: *1dc, skip 1, 1dc. *6 times. (12sts)

19th round: *1dc, skip 1. *6 times. (6sts)

Fasten off.

Body

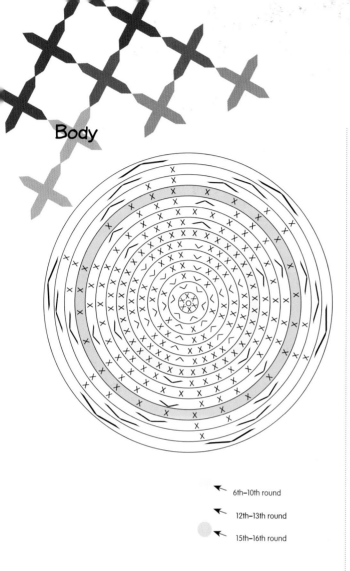

← 6th–10th round

← 12th–13th round

← 15th–16th round

Mane

Use orange yarn.

Make 36 chains.

1st row: *1ch, 5dc into the first st, skip 1. 1dc into next st. Repeat from * to end.

Fasten off.

Arms (need 2)

Use yellow yarn.

Make a loop with the tail end of the yarn on the right, keeping the ball end on the left.

Pull the ball end through the loop. Make one ch through the loop on the hook you have drawn through to steady the circle. 6dc into the circle and join to the first DK with ss to complete.

1st round: *1dc, 2dc. *3 times. (9sts)

Continue to dc for 2in (5cm).

Fasten off.

Finishing

Stuff all parts and sew them together.

Before you stitch the mane onto the body, pin it around first to find the right position.

Embroider the mouth with a scrap of red yarn, and glue on the spiky teeth (white felt).

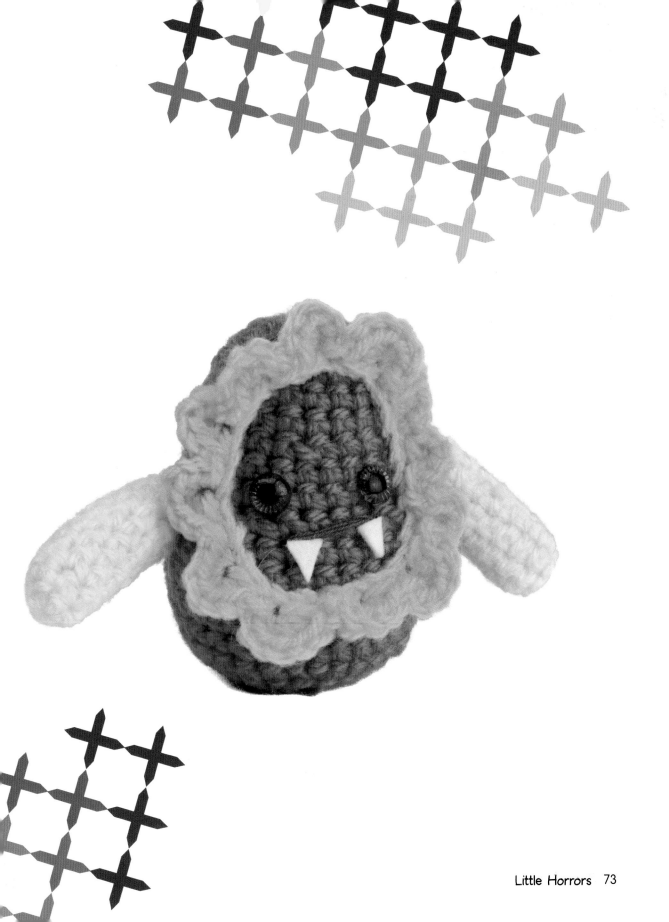

Killer Blob

Lock all your doors and windows – he's coming to get you! Although he may look cute and cuddly, Killer Blob has a split personality, and it's his evil side that's winning! Watch out as he wields the knife and splatters the gore around.

Materials

HOOK SIZE: 4mm

YARN: Orange (DK) Bright Orange (DK)
         Some scraps of red yarn for blood

EYES: 10mm

Body (need 2, front and back)

Make 12ch using orange yarn.

1ch and 1dc all to the end of 12ch, and 2 more dc into the last ch. (Turn.)

1dc back into the first ch. Ss into the first ch to complete.

Next round: 1ch, 3dc into the first dc. 1dc into next 10sts and 3dc into the next dc, 1dc. (Turn.) 3dc into the next dc, 1dc into the next 10sts. 3dc into the next dc, dc into the last dc. Ss to the first ch to complete the round.

Next round: 1dc back to all 12ch to go back to the first dc, 3dc into the next dc, 1dc into the next 12sts. 3dc into the next dc, 1dc, 1dc into the next st to turn. (Turn.) 1dc, 3dc into the next dc, 1dc into the next

12sts, 3dc into the next dc, 1dc, then ss into the first ch to complete the round.

Next round: 1ch, 1dc into next 2dc, 3dc into the next dc. 1dc into the next 14sts, 3dc into the next dc, 1dc into each of next 2dc. 1dc to turn. (Turn.) 1dc into each of next 2dc. 3dc into the next dc. 1dc into each of next 14sts. 3dc into the next dc. 1dc into each of next 2dc. Ss into the first ch to complete the round.

Fasten off.

Make one more.

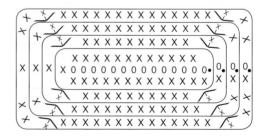

Legs and Arms
(need two each)

Use bright orange yarn.

Make a loop with the tail end of the yarn on the right, keeping the ball end on the left.

Pull the ball end through the loop. Make one ch through the loop on the hook you have drawn through to steady the circle. 6dc into the circle and join to the first DK with ss to complete.

1st round: *1dc, 2dc. *3 times. (9sts)

Continue to dc for 1¼in (3cm).

Fasten off.

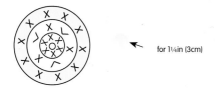

for 1¼in (3cm)

Finishing

Stitch all around the front and back body pieces to join them together. Leave a space unstitched for stuffing. Stuff the monster, and then stitch it closed.

Stuff the other parts and sew them onto the body.

Embroider some blood on the monster's head with the scrap of red yarn.

Zombie Bunny

Be afraid, be very afraid. Zombie Bunny is loose, and he wants you for his own! Look into those staring eyes, give in to his voodoo magic, and he'll soon have you under his spell. Get ready to join the ranks of the living dead . . .

Materials

HOOK SIZE: 4mm

YARN: Green (DK) Orange (DK)

EYES: 9mm

Body

Use green yarn.

Make a loop with the tail end of the yarn on the right, keeping the ball end on the left.

Pull the ball end through the loop. Make one ch through the loop on the hook you have drawn through to steady the circle. 6dc into the circle and join to the first DK with ss to complete.

1st round: 2dc into each of 6dc. (12sts)

2nd round: *1dc. 2dc into next dc. *6 times. (18sts)

3rd round: *1dc into each of next 2dc, 2dc into next dc. *6 times. (24sts)

4th–6th round: *1dc into all sts.

7th round: *1dc into next 6dc, skip 1, 1dc.*3 times. (21sts)

8th round: 1dc into all dc.

9th round: *1dc into next 5dc, skip 1, 1dc. *3 times. (18sts)

10th round: 1dc into all sts.

11th round: *1dc into next 4dc, skip 1, 1dc. *3 times. (15sts)

12th round: 1dc into all dc.

13th round: *1dc into next 3dc. Skip 1, 1dc. *3 times. (12sts)

14th round: *1dc, skip 1. *Repeat for one round.

Fasten off.

Little Horrors 79

4th–6th round

Cheeks (need 2)

Use orange yarn.

6dc into a circle, then ss into the first dc to complete the circle.

Fasten off.

Legs (need 2)

Start the same way as you did for the body (6dc in a circle).

1st round: 2dc into each of 6dc. (12sts)

2nd round: *1dc. 2dc into next dc. *6 times. (18sts)

3rd–6th round: 1dc to all dc.

Fasten off.

Finishing

Stuff all parts and sew them onto the body.

Ears (need 2)

Use orange yarn.

Start the same way as you did for the body (6dc in a circle).

1st round: 2dc into each of 6dc. (12sts)

2nd round: *1dc. 2dc into next dc. *6 times. (18sts)

Continue to dc until the piece is long enough for an ear!

Fasten off.

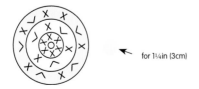

for 1¼in (3cm)

Tiny Ghost

Catch a glimpse of Tiny Ghost and it will send a shiver down your spine. Though she hovers between this world and the beyond, this shy spook really just wants to be friends. So give her a chance and she'll haunt you forever.

Materials

HOOK SIZE: 4mm

YARN: Silver Cotton

EYES: 9mm

Ghost

Use silver cotton yarn.

Make a loop with the tail end of the yarn on the right, keeping the ball end on the left.

Pull the ball end through the loop. Make one ch through the loop on the hook you have drawn through to steady the circle. 6dc into the circle and join to the first DK with ss to complete.

1st round: 2dc into each of 6dc. (12sts)

2nd round: *1dc. 2dc into next dc. *6 times. (18sts)

3rd round: *1dc into next 2dc, 2dc into the next dc. *6 times. (24sts)

4th–10th round: 1dc into all sts.

11th round: *Make 3ch and ss into the next dc. *Repeat for a round.

Fasten off.

With the same yarn, crochet a disc to close the bottom of the body.

Stuff the body and sew on the disc to close the bottom.

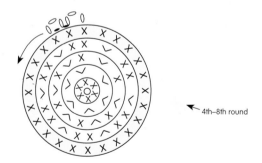

4th–8th round

Cute Pumpkin

Come Halloween, it's Cute Pumpkin's turn to terrorise the neighbourhood. Don't cross her when it comes time to trick-or-treat or she may do a very bad thing indeed. You wouldn't want to suffer the curse of the crazy pumpkin head, would you?

Materials

HOOK SIZE: 4mm

YARN: Orange (DK) Green (DK)

EYES: 9mm

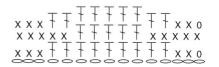

Pumpkin

Work in back loop only.

Using orange yarn, make 16 ch.

1st row: 1dc into 2nd ch from hook. 1dc into next 2ch, htr into next 9ch, 1dc into each of last 3ch. 1ch to start next row.

Turn 2nd row: 1dc into next 5sts. 1htr into next 5sts. 1dc into next 5sts. 1ch to start next row.

Turn 3rd row: 1dc into next 3sts. 1htr into next 9sts. 1dc into next 3sts.

4th–25th row: Repeat 2nd and 3rd row 11 times.

Fasten off.

Stalk

Use green yarn.

Make a loop with the tail end of the yarn on the right, keeping the ball end on the left.

Pull the ball end through the loop. Make one ch through the loop on the hook you have drawn through to steady the circle. 6dc into the circle and join to the first DK with ss to complete.

1st round: *Make 3ch and ss into the next dc. *Repeat for one round.

Fasten off.

Finishing

Stuff the pumpkin and stitch the stalk on top.

Chapter 4
Terrors
in the Wild

Ninja Bear

Battle-scarred Ninja Bear is a martial arts expert and master of disguise. Watch out for his special shape-shifting skills as he disappears into the bamboo grove. Be careful in case this woolly warrior uses his scary-cute powers on you . . .

Materials

HOOK SIZE: 4mm

YARN: Yellow (DK) Blue (DK) Orange (DK)

EYES: 9mm

Body

Use yellow yarn.

Make a loop with the tail end of the yarn on the right, keeping the ball end on the left.

Pull the ball end through the loop. Make one ch through the loop on the hook you have drawn through to steady the circle. 6dc into the circle and join to the first DK with ss to complete.

1st round: 2dc into each of 6dc. (12sts)

2nd round: *1dc. 2dc into next dc. *6 times. (18sts)

3rd round: *1dc into each of next 2dc, 2dc into next dc. *6 times. (24sts)

4th–17th round: 1dc into all sts.

18th round: *1dc into each of next 2dc, skip 1, 1dc into next st. *6 times. (18sts)

19th round: *1dc, skip 1, 1dc into next st. *6 times. (12 sts)

20th round: *1dc, skip 1. *6 times. (6sts)

Fasten off.

Head

Use yellow yarn.

Start in the same way you did for the body (6dc into a circle).

1st round: 2dc into each of 6dc. (12sts)

2nd round: *1dc. 2dc into next dc. *6 times. (18sts)

3rd round: *1dc into each of next 2dc, 2dc into next dc. *6 times. (24sts)

4th round: *1dc into each of next 3dc, 2dc into next dc. *6 times. (30sts)

5th–8th round: 1dc into all dc.

9th round: *1dc into each of next 3dc, skip 1, 1dc. *6 times. (24sts)

10th round: *1dc into each of next 2dc, skip 1, 1dc. *6 times. (18sts)

11th round: *1dc, skip 1, 1dc. *6 times. (12sts)

12th round: *1dc, skip 1. *6 times. (6sts)

Fasten off.

Legs (need 2)

Use yellow yarn.

Start in the same way as you did to make the body, making a circle with 6dc.

1st round: 2dc into each of 6dc. (12sts)

Continue to dc for 1¼in (3cm).

Fasten off.

Arms (need 2)

Use yellow yarn.

Start in the same way, making a circle with 6dc.

1st round: 2dc into each of 6dc. (12sts)

Continue to dc for 2in (5cm).

Fasten off.

Ears (need 2)

Use yellow yarn.

Start in the same way, but make 3dc into a circle instead of 6dc.

1st round: 2dc into each of 3dc. (6sts)

Continue to dc for 2 rounds.

Fasten off.

Cheeks (need 2)

Use orange yarn.

6dc into a circle then ss into the first dc to complete the circle.

Fasten off.

Eye Patch

Use blue yarn.

6dc into a circle then ss into the first dc to complete the circle.

Fasten off.

Attach some ch sts to the patch.

Finishing

Stuff the head and the body, and then sew all parts together.

Nasty Bug

It's spring, when all the Nasty Bugs swarm, and this one's just emerged from his cocoon. Check all the nooks and crannies in your home with care, or you'll end up with a plague of cute critters no exterminator can cure.

Materials

HOOK SIZE: 4mm

YARN: Orange (DK) Pink (DK) Blue (DK)

EYES: 9mm

Head

Use orange yarn.

Make a loop with the tail end of the yarn on the right, keeping the ball end on the left.

Pull the ball end through the loop. Make one ch through the loop on the hook you have drawn through to steady the circle. 6dc into the circle and join to the first DK with ss to complete.

1st round: 2dc into each of 6dc. (12sts)

2nd round: *1dc. 2dc into next dc. *6 times. (18sts)

3rd round: *1dc into each of next 2dc, 2dc into next dc. *6 times. (24sts)

4th–15th round: *1dc into all sts.

16th round: *1dc into each of next 2dc, skip 1, 1dc into next st. *6 times. (18sts)

17th round: *1dc, skip 1, 1dc into next st. *6 times. (12sts)

18th round: *1dc, skip 1. *6 times. (6sts)

Fasten off.

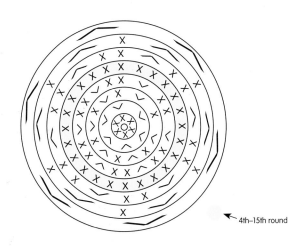

4th–15th round

Legs (need 2)

Use pink or blue yarn.

Make a loop with the tail end of the yarn on the right, keeping the ball end on the left.

Pull the ball end through the loop. Make one ch through the loop on the hook you have drawn through to steady the circle. 6dc into the circle and join to the first DK with ss to complete.

1st round: 2dc into each of 6dc. (12sts)

2nd round: *1dc. 2dc into next dc. *6 times. (18sts)

Continue to dc for 1½in (4cm).

Fasten off.

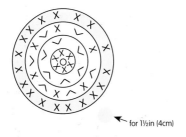

← for 1½in (4cm)

Finishing

Stuff all parts and stitch all of them together.

Bad Bunny

This naughty rabbit is rotten to the core, and he's been up to no good. Forget the idea of cute-and-fluffy little bunnikins, it's no more Mr. Nice Guy now. This Bad Bunny has been a very bad boy indeed!

Materials

HOOK SIZE: 4mm

YARN: Pink (DK) Purple (DK) Blue (DK) Yellow (DK)

EYES: 6mm

Head

Use purple yarn.

Make a loop with the tail end of the yarn on the right, keeping the ball end on the left.

Pull the ball end through the loop. Make one ch through the loop on the hook you have drawn through to steady the circle. 6dc into the circle and join to the first DK with ss to complete.

1st round: 2dc into each of 6dc. (12sts)

2nd round: *1dc. 2dc into next dc. *6 times. (18sts)

3rd round: *1dc into each of next 2dc, 2dc into next dc. *6 times. (24sts)

4th–7th round: 1dc into all sts.

8th round: *1dc into each of next 2dc, skip 1, 1dc. *6 times. (18sts)

9th round: Change the yarn to blue. *1dc, skip 1, 1dc. *6 times. (12sts)

10th round: *1dc into each of the next 6dc, skip 1. *6 times. (6sts)

Stuff it.

Fasten off.

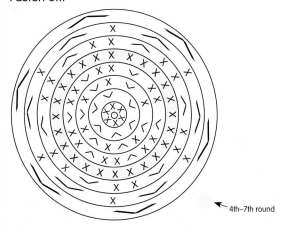

4th–7th round

Body

Use blue yarn.

1st round: 2dc into each of 6dc. (12sts)

2nd round: *1dc. 2dc into next dc. *6 times. (18sts)

3rd round: *1dc into each of next 2dc, 2dc into next dc. *6 times. (24sts)

4th–5th round: 1dc into all sts.

6th–7th round: Change the yarn to yellow. 1dc into all sts.

8th round: *1dc into each of next 2dc, skip 1, 1dc. *6 times. (18sts)

9th round: *1dc, skip 1, 1dc. *6 times. (12sts)

Fasten off.

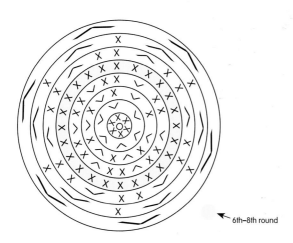

← 6th–8th round

Ears (need 2)

Use pink yarn.

Start the same way as you did for the body, with 6dc in a circle.

1st round: 2dc into each of 6dc. (12sts)

Next round: 1dc into all dc for 1½–2in (4–5cm).

Fasten off.

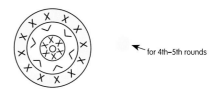

← for 4th–5th rounds

Tail

Use pink yarn.

Start the same way as you did for the body (6dc in a circle).

1st round: 2dc into each of 6dc.

2nd round: 1dc into all dc for 2 rounds.

Fasten off.

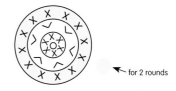

← for 2 rounds

Legs (need 2)

Use blue yarn.

1st round: *1dc into next dc, 2dc into next st. *3 times. (9sts)

1dc into all sts for 3 rounds. Fasten off.

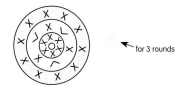

← for 3 rounds

Finishing

Stuff all parts and sew them onto the body.

Creepy Crawly

It's time to start worrying if you get an infestation of this Creepy Crawly. When a crazy caterpillar like this transforms, who knows what mad, mutant insect might appear? It could be a beautiful butterfly, but it might just as well be a monstrous moth.

Materials

HOOK SIZE: 4mm

YARN: Turquoise (DK) Orange (DK) Pink (DK) Green (DK)

Scraps of yarn for cheeks and hat

EYES: 6mm

Head-Body (need 4)

(For a longer monster make more balls. Be sure to use different coloured yarn for each one).

Use pink yarn.

Make a loop with the tail end of the yarn on the right, keeping the ball end on the left.

Pull the ball end through the loop. Make one ch through the loop on the hook you have drawn through to steady the circle. 6dc into the circle and join to the first DK with ss to complete.

1st round: 2dc into each of 6dc. (12sts)

2nd round: *1dc. 2dc into next dc. *6 times. (18sts)

3rd round: *1dc into each of next 2dc, 2dc into next dc. *6 times. (24sts)

4th–6th round: 1dc into every dc.

7th round: *1dc into each of next 2dc, skip 1, 1dc. *6 times. (18sts)

8th round: *1dc, skip 1, 1dc. *6 times. (12sts)

9th round: 1dc into all sts, skipping alternate dc. (6sts)

Fasten off.

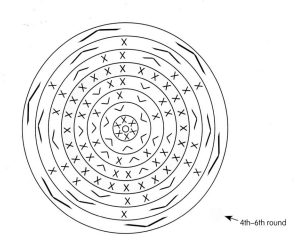

4th–6th round

Cheeks (need 2)

Use scraps of yarn.

6dc into a circle, then ss into the first dc to complete the circle.

Fasten off.

Hat

Use blue yarn.

6dc into a circle, then ss into the first dc to complete the circle.

1dc into all 6dc for 3 rounds.

Fasten off.

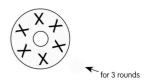

for 3 rounds

Finishing

Stuff each part and join all of the balls together.

Poison Mushroom

She may look as pretty as a picture, but Poison Mushroom is totally toxic. This foul fungus lurks on the forest floor, luring unsuspecting victims with her rosy red cap. But don't be tempted: picking her up may be the last thing you do . . .

Materials

HOOK SIZE: 4mm

YARN: Pale Yellow (DK) Red (DK)
Moss Green (DK)

EYES: 9mm

Top

Use red yarn.

Make a loop with the tail end of the yarn on the right, keeping the ball end on the left.

Pull the ball end through the loop. Make one ch through the loop on the hook you have drawn through to steady the circle. 6dc into the circle and join to the first DK with ss to complete.

1st round: 1dc, 2dc into the next sts. *3 times. (9sts)

2nd round: *1dc into each of next 2dc, 2dc into the next dc. *3 times. (12sts)

3rd round: *1dc into each of next 2dc, 2dc into the next dc. *4 times. (16sts)

4th round: *1dc into each of next 3dc, 2dc into the next dc. *4 times. (20sts)

5th round: *1dc into each of next 4dc, 2dc into the next dc.*4 times. (24sts)

Fasten off.

Use yellow yarn to make a bottom for the mushroom cap.

Start in the same way as you did for the top (a circle with 6dc).

1st round: 2dc into each of 6dc. (12sts)

2nd round: *1dc. 2dc into next dc. *6 times. (18sts)

3rd round: *1dc into each of next 2dc, 2dc into next dc. *6 times. (24sts)

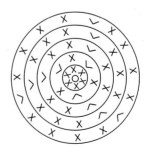

Body

Use yellow yarn.

Start in the same way as you did for the top (6dc in a circle).

1st round: 2dc into each of 6dc. (12sts)

2nd round: *1dc. 2dc into next dc. *6 times. (18sts)

3rd round: *1dc into each of next 2dc, 2dc into next dc. *6 times. (24sts)

4th–5th round: 1dc into all sts. (24sts)

6th round: *1dc into each of next 4sts, skip 1, 1dc. *4 times. (20sts)

7th round: *1dc into each of next 3sts, skip 1, 1dc. *4 times. (16sts)

8th round: 1dc into all sts.

Fasten off.

Finishing

Using moss green yarn, French knot on the top for a mouldy effect.

Stuff all parts and sew them together.

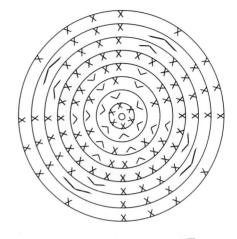

4th–5th round

Chapter 5
Friendly Freaks

Happy Devil

Why is Happy Devil so happy? Well, he knows how easy it is to lead you astray. No matter how hard you try to resist, all it takes is one scary-cute wave and a cheeky wink, and you'll readily follow his bad example.

Materials

HOOK SIZE: 4mm

YARN: Turquoise (DK)   Orange (DK)   Lemon (DK)
        Bright orange scraps for horns and cheeks

EYES: 6mm

Head

Use turquoise yarn. Make a loop with the tail end of the yarn on the right, keeping the ball end on the left.

Pull the ball end through the loop. Make one ch through the loop on the hook you have drawn through to steady the circle. 6dc into the circle and join to the first DK with ss to complete.

1st round: 2dc into each of 6dc. (12sts)

2nd round: *1dc. 2dc into next dc. *6 times. (18sts)

3rd round: *1dc into each of next 2dc, 2dc into next dc. *6 times. (24sts)

4th–7th round: 1dc into every dc.

8th round: *1dc into each of next 2dc, skip 1, 1dc. *6 times. (18sts)

9th round: *1dc, skip 1, 1dc. *6 times. (12sts)

10th–11th round: 1dc into every dc.

12th round: *1dc, skip 1. *6 times. (6sts)

Fasten off.

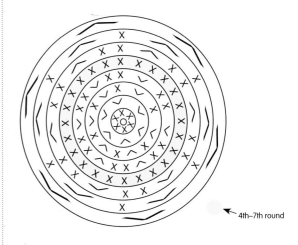

4th–7th round

Body

Use turquoise yarn. Start in the same way as you did with the head (6dc into a circle).

1st round: 2dc into each of 6dc. (12sts)

2nd round: *1dc. 2dc into next dc. *6 times. (18sts)

3rd round: *1dc into every dc. (18sts)

4th round: *1dc into each of next 2dc, 2dc into next dc. *6 times. (24sts)

5th round: 1dc into every dc. (24sts)

6th round: *1dc into each of next 3dc, 2dc into next dc. *6 times. (30sts)

7th–9th round: 1dc into every dc.

10th round: *1dc into each of next 3dc, skip 1, 1dc. *6 times. (24sts)

11th–12th round: 1dc into every dc.

13th round: *1dc into next 2dc, skip 1, 1dc. *6 times. (18sts)

14th round: *1dc into next dc, skip 1, 1dc. *6 times. (12sts)

Fasten off.

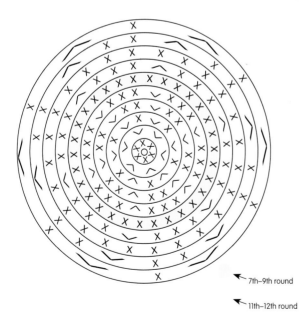

7th–9th round

11th–12th round

Arms (need 2)

(Try to make one of them stripy.)

Use orange yarn. Make a loop with the tail end of the yarn on the right, keeping the ball end on the left.

Pull the ball end through the loop. Make one ch through the loop on the hook you have drawn through to steady the circle. 6dc into the circle and join to the first DK with ss to complete.

1st round: *1dc into next dc, 2dc into next dc. *3 times. (9sts)

1dc into all for 2in (5cm), then fasten off. (Change colour every 2 rounds for the stripy arm).

Legs (need 2)

Start the same way you did for the arms, but 2dc into each of 6dc (12sts) and then 1dc into all sts for 1¾in (4.5cm).

Fasten off.

Tummy

Use bright orange (ideally slightly fluffy yarn, such as mohair). Start in the same 6dc-in-a-circle way.

1st round: 2dc into each of 6dc. (12sts)

2nd round: *1dc. 2dc into next dc. *6 times. (18sts)

3rd round: *1dc into each of next 2dc, 2dc into next dc. *6 times. (24sts)

4th round: *1dc into each of next 3dc, 2dc into next dc.*6 times. (30sts)

5th round: *1dc into each of next 4dc, 2dc into next dc. *6 times. (36sts)

6th round: 1dc into all sts.

Fasten off.

Horns (need 2)

Use bright orange yarn. Make 6 ch and ss into the first ch to form a circle.

1dc into each ch for 3 rounds.

1dc, skip 1, 1dc. Twice. (4sts)

1dc into all sts for another 2 rounds.

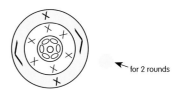

for 2 rounds

Finishing

Stuff all parts and sew them onto the body.

Cheeks (need 2)

Use orange yarn. 6dc into a circle, then ss into the first dc to complete the circle.

Fasten off.

Repeat instructions with yellow yarn for the nose.

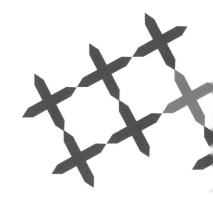

Little Round Thing

Can you unravel the mystery of Little Round Thing? What kind of creature is he – a ball of fun or an evil blob? Just when you think you've got a grip on him, he'll morph into a weird and woolly freak.

Materials

HOOK SIZE: 4mm

YARN: Pink (DK)   Green (DK)   Eggy Yellow (DK)   Baby Green (DK)

EYES: 9mm

Head-Body

Use pink yarn. Make a loop with the tail end of the yarn on the right, keeping the ball end on the left.

Pull the ball end through the loop. Make one ch through the loop on the hook you have drawn through to steady the circle. 6dc into the circle and join to the first DK with ss to complete.

1st round: 2dc into each of 6dc. (12sts)

2nd round: *1dc. 2dc into next dc. *6 times. (18sts)

3rd round: *1dc into each of next 2dc, 2dc into next dc. *6 times. (24sts)

4th–6th round: 1dc into all sts.

7th round: *1dc into each of next 2dc, skip 1, 1dc. *6 times. (18sts)

8th round: Change the yarn to green. *1dc, skip 1, 1dc. *6 times. (12sts)

9th round: 1dc into all sts, skipping alternate dc. (6sts)

Stuff the body.

Fasten off.

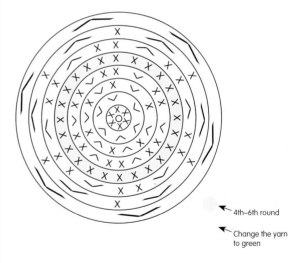

4th–6th round

Change the yarn to green

Arms (need 2)

Use baby green yarn (eggy yellow for one side). Make a loop with the tail end of the yarn on the right, keeping the ball end on the left.

Pull the ball end through the loop. Make one ch through the loop on the hook you have drawn through to steady the circle. 6dc into the circle and join to the first DK with ss to complete.

1st round: *1dc into next dc, 2dc into next dc. *3 times. (9sts)

1dc into all sts for 1½in (4cm), then fasten off.

Legs (need 2)

Use baby green yarn (eggy yellow for one side).

Repeat the instructions for the arms, but make them slightly longer.

1st round: *1dc into next dc, 2dc into next dc. *3 times. (9sts)

1dc into all sts for 2in (5cm), then fasten off.

Finishing

Stuff all parts and sew them together.

Strange Pet

This dinky little dinosaur might seem like the perfect freaky friend for you. But don't be taken in by Strange Pet's winsome ways – she can switch from cute-and-crazy reptile to terrible lizard in the blink of an eye.

Materials

HOOK SIZE: 4mm

YARN: Green (DK)   Pink (DK)   Orange (DK)

EYES: 4mm

Body

Use green yarn. Make a loop with the tail end of the yarn on the right, keeping the ball end on the left.

Pull the ball end through the loop. Make one ch through the loop on the hook you have drawn through to steady the circle. 6dc into the circle and join to the first DK with ss to complete.

1st round: 2dc into each of 6dc. (12sts)

2nd round: *1dc. 2dc into next dc. *6 times. (18sts)

3rd round: *1dc into each of next 2dc, 2dc into next dc. *6 times. (24sts)

4th–6th round: 1dc into all sts.

7th round: *1dc into each of next 2dc, skip 1, 1dc into next dc. *6 times. (18sts)

8th round: *1dc, skip 1, 1dc into next dc. *6 times. (12sts)

9th round: *1dc, skip 1. *6 times. (6sts)

Fasten off.

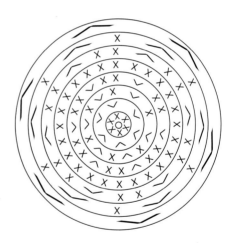

Neck

Start in the same way you did for the body.

1st round: 2dc into each of 6dc. (12sts)

2nd round: *1dc. 2dc into next dc. *6 times. (18sts)

Continue to dc until the neck is long enough.

Next round: *1dc, skip 1, 1dc. *6 times. (12sts)

Fasten off.

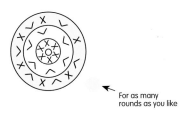

← For as many rounds as you like

← 4th–5th round

Head

Use green yarn. Make a loop with the tail end of the yarn on the right, keeping the ball end on the left.

Pull the ball end through the loop. Make one ch through the loop on the hook you have drawn through to steady the circle. 6dc into the circle and join to the first DK with ss to complete.

1st round: 2dc into each of 6dc. (12sts)

2nd round: *1dc. 2dc into next dc. *6 times. (18sts)

3rd round: *1dc into each of next 2dc, 2dc into next dc. *6 times. (24sts)

4th–5th round: *1dc into all sts.

6th round: *1dc into each of next 2dc, skip 1, 1dc into next dc. *6 times. (18sts)

7th round: *1dc, skip 1, 1dc into next dc. *6 times. (12sts)

8th round: *1dc, skip 1. *6 times. (12sts)

Fasten off.

Legs (need 4)

Use pink yarn. Start in the same way you did for the head (6dc in a circle).

1st round: *1dc, 2dc. *3 times. (9sts)

Continue to dc for ¾in (2cm).

Fasten off.

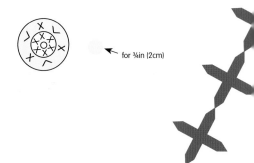

← for ¾in (2cm)

Hat

Use orange yarn.

Use the 6dc-in-a-circle method to start.

1st round: 2dc into each of 6dc. (12sts)

2nd–3rd round: 1dc into all dc.

4th round: *1dc, 2dc into next st. *6 times. (18sts)

5th round: *1dc into each of next 2dc. 2dc into next st. *6 times. (24sts)

Fasten off.

← for 2 rounds

Tail

Make 6 ch and join the first ch with ss to form a circle.

1dc into each of 6 ch for 3 rounds.

1dc into every alternate dc (3sts).

Fasten off.

Finishing

Stuff all parts and sew them onto the body.

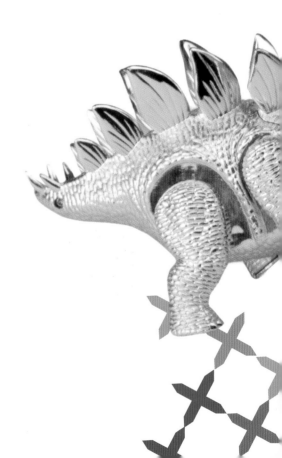

Weird Blue Boy

Different things frighten different people, so what gives you goosebumps? Will Weird Blue Boy be your personal bogeyman? Do his googly eyes give you the willies? Or does this overalls-clad deviant just make you want to giggle?

Materials

HOOK SIZE: 4mm

YARN: Sky Blue (DK) Red (DK) White (DK)

EYES: 9mm

Legs (need 2)

Use red yarn. Make a loop with the tail end of the yarn on the right, keeping the ball end on the left.

Pull the ball end through the loop. Make one ch through the loop on the hook you have drawn through to steady the circle. 6dc into the circle and join to the first DK with ss to complete.

1st round: 2dc into each of 6dc. (12sts)

2nd–4th round: *1dc into all dc. (12sts)

Change yarn to white.

1dc into all dc for 2 rounds.

Change yarn to red.

1dc into all dc for 2 rounds.

Change yarn to white.

1dc into all dc for 2 rounds.

Change yarn to red and dc for another 3 rounds.

Fasten off.

Body

Stitch 2 tubes (legs) together. (See illustration on p.132).

Pick up 24sts from top of the legs.

1dc into each dc for 5 rounds using red yarn.

Change yarn to sky blue.

1dc into each dc for 6 rounds.

*1dc into each of next 2dc, skip 1, 1dc. *6 times. (18sts)

*1dc, skip 1, 1dc. *6 times. (12sts)

*1dc into every alternate st. (6sts)

Stuff the body and fasten off.

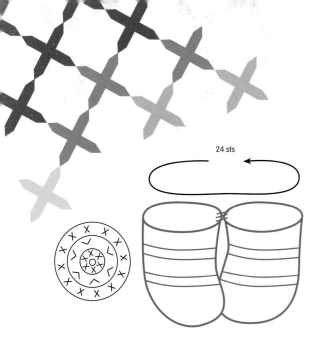

24 sts

Hat

Use a scrap of red yarn to 6dc into a circle, as usual.

2dc into each dc. (12dc).

1dc into all sts, then fasten off.

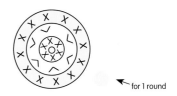

← for 1 round

Arms (need 2)

Use sky blue yarn. Make a loop with the tail end of the yarn on the right, keeping the ball end on the left.

Pull the ball end through the loop. Make one ch through the loop on the hook you have drawn through to steady the circle. 6dc into the circle and join to the first DK with ss to complete.

1st round: *1dc into next dc, 2dc into next dc. *3 times. (9sts)

1dc into all sts for 2in (5cm), then fasten off.

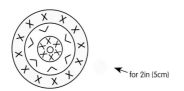

← for 2in (5cm)

Finishing

Stuff all parts, and stitch the arms onto the body.

Chain stitch around the arms for the overalls straps.

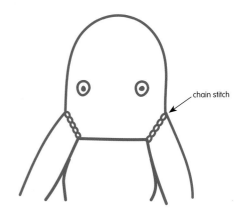

chain stitch

Pointy-head Girl

From the land of fairytale and fable comes the weird but wonderful Pointy-head Girl. This mixed-up minx could be the last survivor of those mythical one-horned monsters – or just a scary-cute experiment gone horribly wrong . . .

Materials

HOOK SIZE: 4mm

YARN: Green (DK) Purple (DK) Orange (DK)
       Yellow (DK)

EYES: 6mm

Head

Use green yarn. Make a loop with the tail end of the yarn on the right, keeping the ball end on the left.

Pull the ball end through the loop. Make one ch through the loop on the hook you have drawn through to steady the circle. 6dc into the circle and join to the first DK with ss to complete.

1st round: 2dc into each of 6dc. (12sts)

2nd round: *1dc. 2dc into next dc. *6 times. (18sts)

3rd round: *1dc into each of next 2dc, 2dc into next dc. *6 times. (24sts)

4th–6th round: 1dc into all sts.

7th round: *1dc into each of next 2dc, skip 1, 1dc. *6 times. (18sts)

8th round: *1dc, skip 1, 1dc. *6 times. (12sts)

9th round: 1dc into all sts, skipping alternate dc. (6sts)

Stuff the head and fasten off.

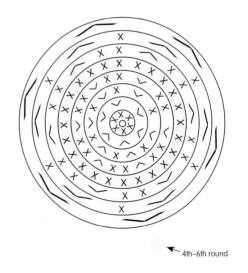

4th–6th round

Body

Use purple yarn. Start the same way as you did for the head (a circle with 6dc).

1st round: 2dc into each of 6dc. (12sts)

2nd round: *1dc. 2dc into next dc. *6 times. (18sts)

3rd–7th round: 1dc into all sts.

8th round: *1dc into each of next 4dc, skip 1, 1dc. *3 times. (15sts)

1dc into all sts for next 3 rounds.

Fasten off.

Arms/Legs (need 2 of each)

Use orange yarn.

Start in the same way as you did for the head (a circle with 6dc).

Continue to dc for 1¼in (3cm), then fasten off.

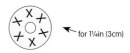

← for 1¼in (3cm)

Horn

Use yellow yarn.

Make 6 ch and join the first ch with ss to form a circle.

1dc into each of 6 ch for 3 rounds.

1dc into every alternate dc (3sts).

Fasten off.

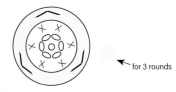

← for 3 rounds

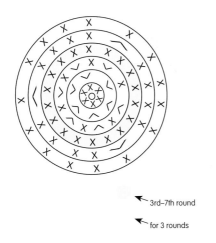

← 3rd–7th round

← for 3 rounds

Finishing

Stuff all parts and sew them onto the body.

Monsters Index

Resources

Enter the scary-cute world of amigurumi. The following tried and tested retailers and suppliers can help you on your mission to fill your life with cuteness.

UK

Angel Yarns UK

www.angelyarns.com

Knitshop

www.knitshop.co.uk

Knit and Sew

www.knitandsew.co.uk

Laughing Hens

www.laughinghens.com

Loop Yarn Shop

www.loop.gb.com

Mason's Needlecraft

www.masonsneedlecraft.co.uk

Prick Your Finger

www.prickyourfinger.com

International

Blue Sky Alpacas, Inc

www.blueskyalpacas.com

Koigu Wool Designs

www.koigu.com

Patons

www.patonsyarns.com

Useful Information

If you are stuck for an idea or missing tools and materials, there is a serious online community support network of crochet and amigurumi enthusiasts. Check out The Knitting and Crochet Guild of the UK (www.knitting-and-crochet-guild.org) and Crochet Australia (www.crochetaustralia.com.au) for crochet news, links to resources, and tips and advice. Try Etsy (www.etsy.com) for patterns, accessories, books, and all your other amigurumi needs.

Index